Matters of the Heart

PATIENCE SAKUTUKWA

Navigating Heartbreaks through shared experiences

Matters of the Heart Edition 2

Copyright ©2021, 2024 by Patience Sakutukwa

ISBN: 978-0-7961-5298-5

Edited by – Bethel Publishing House

Typesetting & Layout by – Malebo Semosa

Cover Design- Lindani L. Thango

Printed by Creative Books S.A. & Printdoctor

Printed in South Africa

Scripture and quotation are taken from:

AMPC 1987. The Lockman Foundation

KJV Cambridge. University Press

ESV.2001. Crossway. Good News Publishers

NLT. 2015 Tyndale House Foundation. Illinois

MSG .2018 Eugene H. Peterson

CONTENTS

ACKNOWLEDGMENTS

I am profoundly grateful to all those with whom I've had the pleasure of collaborating during the creation of this book. Among them, none has been more significant than the Holy Spirit, who stands as my closest companion and friend. In His essence, He inspired me not only to share my own life experiences but also those of my esteemed colleagues. These narratives delve into matters of the heart and relationships in general. Thank you, Holy Spirit, my forever faithful Friend; your love and guidance accompany me in every endeavor. You serve as my ultimate role model. I extend my sincere appreciation to the dedicated team behind this project, whose tireless efforts transformed this endeavor into a reality. It was truly a pleasure working with you and a valuable learning experience throughout the process.

DEDICATION

I dedicate this book to all those who have experienced hurt, brokenness, wounds, betrayal, and disappointments by individuals who masked and disguised themselves as saviors. I honor your courage; I love you and remember, God loves you even more.

The Spirit of the Sovereign Lord is upon me because the Lord has appointed me to bring good news to the poor. He has sent me to comfort the broken-hearted and to announce that captives will be released and prisoners will be freed. 2. He has sent me to tell those who mourn that the time of the Lord's favor has come, and with it, the day of God's anger against their enemies.

3. To all who mourn in Israel, he will give beauty for ashes, joy instead of mourning, and praise instead of despair. For the Lord has planted them like strong and graceful oaks for His glory.

~ Isaiah 61:1-3 NLT

FOREWORD

He heals the broken-hearted and bandages their wounds.

- Psalm 147:3 NLT

Patience shares her journey from heartache to healing in an unfeigned manner in 'Matters of the Heart'.

May her testimony be a beacon of hope to many.

Pastor Charné Pretorius

PREFACE

Welcome to Matters of the Heart Edition 2—a little adventure into the ups and downs of relationships. Imagine it as a cozy chat about love, heartache, and all the messy, wonderful stuff in between. So, why Edition 2? Well, this time around, it's not just my tales of love gone haywire. I roped in some buddies, and together, we spilled the beans on our relationship rollercoasters. It's like a group therapy session, but way more fun.

As you flip through these pages, you'll catch glimpses of our real-life love dramas. No filters, just genuine stories about the struggles and triumphs of trying to make love work.

Think of this book as your buddy, your go-to when you're knee-deep in relationship puzzles. We're all in this together, sharing a few laughs, shedding a few tears, and learning a thing or two about the crazy adventure called love.

So, grab a cup of coffee, cozy up, and let's dive into Matters of the Heart Edition 2. It's not just a book; it's a friendly chat about love—messy, complicated, but always worth it.

INTRODUCTION

In the intricate tapestry of life, we often find ourselves entangled in the labyrinth of heartaches and heartbreaks. Our focus tends to fixate on the turbulent landscape of romantic relationships. Yet, the tendrils of emotional turmoil can infiltrate any connection, be it with friends, siblings, or even those we regard as guardians and

protectors.

My journey through the corridors of pain extended beyond the confines of a typical broken heart. It comprised a trilogy of abuses—verbal, sexual, and emotional—perpetrated by individuals I once held in high esteem. I believed these people were meant to be my safeguards, nurturers, and up lifters.

Instead, they etched horrifying moments into the canvas of my life, moments that would echo through the corridors of my consciousness for years to come. Leaving behind a broken heart when the person designated to protect you inflicts unimaginable harm changes you.

Pain becomes a chisel, carving out a new understanding of the world, marred by betrayal, vulnerability, and shattered trust. In the aftermath of abuse, something within us transforms. It's not merely the breaking of the heart; it's the fracturing of the very essence of one's being.

Yet, as I pen down these words for the world to read, I understand that it signify more than a narrative of torment. It's a testament to conquering the pain, to healing, and to recovery—all in the embrace of Christ.

In the wake of this hurtful robbery of innocence, I've emerged not as a victim but as a survivor, standing on the solid ground of my faith and the resilience it imparts. When you endure abuse, something changes irreversibly. Pain is a force that molds, sculpts, and, in the crucible of adversity, forges a new version of you.

This is my journey from the ashes of abuse, a journey that I share not to solicit pity but to illuminate the path of healing, strength, and restoration for those who may have traversed or are currently traversing similar dark terrains.

Together, we will explore the metamorphosis that occurs when pain changes you, and how, in Christ, we find the source of our renewal and restoration.

In the aftermath of the abuses I endured, I found myself in a state of fragility—a delicate emotional tapestry easily torn by the slightest touch. The scars of my past have rendered me acutely sensitive to the world around me.

Even the most innocuous gestures or fleeting touches can send shockwaves through my being, resurrecting the haunting echoes of my traumatic experiences.

It's as if my emotional skin, once resilient, has become fragile, susceptible to the gentlest breeze of human interaction. Divorce, separations, death, life-threatening illnesses, abuse, and mental un-wellness can be like sailing across an endless ocean when you are anchored in faith. Picture yourself in a sailboat, surrounded by an expanse of sea with no land in sight. Imagine the prospect of days passing without even the possibility of spotting land, providing you with the opportunity to once again stand at the helm of your destiny and rectify every misstep.

We all yearn for that elusive second chance to mend relationships we may have traversed, leaving loose ends in our wake. A desire lingers for another moment in the garden with our cherished ones—perhaps watching lilies bloom or sharing a quiet coffee. It's a chance to reconcile where we may have spoken at cross purposes, driven by ignorance, bitterness, anger, or even envy.

We've all experienced those moments in life when it feels as if we're sailing across an endless ocean, unsure if land will ever appear on the horizon. These are times marked by fractured relationships of various kinds, leaving a profound impact on our hearts.

Whether it's unhealthy connections or the failure to nurture the right ones that God has placed in our lives for growth, the toll is deep. The conclusion of a relationship, particularly one marked by profound love, often leads to mutual sadness in the unforeseen final chapter. You may have been collaborating, setting goals, and impacting society as a team— serving together in the house of God and sharpening one another. Some connections are undeniably heaven-sent, God-given alliances. Yet, abruptly, the honeymoon phase concludes, leaving you bewildered at how you arrived at a point of hurting each other.

It's disheartening when relationships, be they colleagues, friends, business partners, or spouses, evolve into a state of being strangers—today allies, tomorrow enemies. The world, complex and muddied by human nature, becomes a challenging place. In such moments, you reflect on the efforts you've invested in loved ones, bending over backward for them, only for them to decide to sever ties. You ponder whether they are oblivious to the enemy's work in separating divine connections or if they lack the strength to endure your flaws. Perhaps impatience prevails, and they fail to grasp the demands of patience in fostering connection.

Have you ever questioned if you are the one prematurely walking away from undeniably divine connections? I've trodden that path, feeling compelled to disconnect from connections whose burdens seemed too heavy. However, I admit regret for severing ties with connections that were undoubtedly God-ordained. Opportunities were lost due to hasty judgments and premature conclusions.

In those moments, wisdom is paramount. The Holy Spirit becomes our guide, delving into the depth of matters and aligning our souls and physical beings. After experiencing the pain of broken relationships, I sought the Holy Spirit's discernment and counsel. Instead of pointing fingers at others, I turned the scrutiny inward, asking God for patience and understanding.

I became curious about my own shortcomings, eager to understand and rectify them, preserving every

1

divine connection God brought into my life. The Holy Spirit revealed the importance of community, even for an introvert like me. Recognizing the need for others around me became a crucial step in navigating the complexities of relationships.

"Iron sharpeneth iron; so a man sharpened the countenance of his friend."

Proverbs 27:17 KJV

"To be 'in the will of God is not a matter of intellectual discernment, but a state of heart." **Oswald Chambers** *"The only way to break the chains of fear and doubt is to know in your heart that God loves you no matter what."* **Joyce Meyer**

"The Christian faith is ultimately not only a matter of doctrine or understanding or of intellect, it is a condition of the heart." **David Lloyd-Jones**

"God *began to deal with me...As the tears rolled down my face, God said, You are thinking like a man. You are always concerned about the outward appearance...but what is the condition of your heart*

1

toward me and toward My people? I sat there confused and said to the Lord, 'MY HEART?'..." **Dr Juanita Bynum**

"I feel the matter of my heart being transformed, metallized, in an optimism of steel." **Filippo Tommaso Marinetti**

"You can't be striving to please; you must be striving to get to the heart of the matter." **Vanessa Redgrave**

"If you look at the people in your circle and don't get inspired then you don't have a circle, you have a cage." **Mel Robbins**

"As long as a man has a golden heart, it does not matter whether he has green blood or blue skin!" **Mehmet Murat ildan**

"No matter how much tarnish you think is on the tabernacle of your heart, you still shine because of God's love." **Mark R. Woodward**

"It doesn't matter what size you are. It matters how big your heart is and how smart you are." **Freddy Adu**

1

CHAPTER 1

RELATIONSHIP REALITIES

"And I will ask the Father, and He will give you another Helper (Comforter, Advocate, Intercessor—Counselor, Strengthener, Standby), to be with you forever." - John
14:16 AMP

As you navigate through life, a battle unfolds in your heart—a clash of emotions fueled by anger, frustration, heartbreak, or rejection. Maybe your spouse left, your fiancé ended things, or your parents abandoned you. Perhaps, relationships with your child, siblings, and friends are strained, or you're grappling with the loss of a loved one or battling a life-threatening illness. Regrets may linger from helping ungrateful individuals who left you miserable.

1

It's a common human experience to yearn for a chance to correct past mistakes, to rewind time and handle situations differently. However, the past can't be changed. What's within your control is shaping a different future.

You can't erase heartbreaks, but you have the power to prevent history from repeating itself. We are all works in progress, and admitting it allows us to foster healthier relationships.

This book is not written to offend anyone from past failed relationships—be it business colleagues, ministry associates, friends, family, or any relationship. It's a message directed to those who, like me, have navigated through wrong relationships. The Holy Spirit intervened in my life, and through Matters of the Heart, I share my experiences to reach souls struggling in similar situations.

Relationships lie at the core of life, impacting untimely deaths, mental health, and overall well-being. Whether with partners, friends, children, co-workers, or the world around us, relationships

1

require wisdom and effort to thrive. Expanding our definition of relationships to include various aspects of life is crucial for growing intimacy. Many articles focus on romantic relationships, but all relationships play a role in shaping our hearts.

Through intimacy, honesty, and awareness, relationships become mirrors reflecting our true selves. Productive relationships often involve a power dynamic, such as parent-child, mentor-mentee, or husband-wife, fostering respect and order.

My advice is to choose your companions wisely. As Mel Robbins wisely said, *"If you look at the people in your circle and don't get inspired, then you don't have a circle, you have a cage."* Surround yourself with mentors who inspire and guide you.

To discern right from wrong relationships, categorize people into confidants, comrades, and constituents. Confidants are close, trustworthy individuals who uplift and heal. Comrades are temporary allies aligned against a common foe.

1

Constituents support your cause but may leave when their interests are better served elsewhere. Guard your heart with diligence, as Proverbs 4:23 advises. I learned the hard way, classifying people into these categories to protect my heart and reputation.

Confidants are crucial; comrades are temporary, and constituents may have hidden agendas. Understanding the roles of confidants, comrades, and constituents prevents disappointment. Not everyone is meant to solve your problems; some are there just to celebrate with you. Mastering the art of categorizing people in your life will shield you from disappointment and hurt.

Marriages often stem from successful courtships, but without caution, they lead to heartbreaks and high divorce rates. Carefully choosing a life partner is essential to safeguard your heart. Proverbs 4:23 emphasizes the importance of keeping your heart diligently.

Relationships, involving two or more connected individuals, impact your heart's state. Amos 3:3

1

reinforces the idea that two must agree to walk together. Every relationship contributes to your destiny; hence, relationships should be chosen wisely. While relationships are crucial, the world often overlooks their importance. Entering relationships without understanding their purpose is unwise.

Ask yourself: Is this person here to teach or be taught? To assist or be assisted? God, recognizing the importance of companionship, provided Adam with a helper (Genesis 2:19).

1

CHAPTER 2

HEARTBREAK ENCOUNTERS

"I remembered God, and was troubled: I
complained, and my spirit was overwhelmed. Selah.
Thou holdest mine eyes waking: I am so troubled
that I cannot speak."

- Psalm 77:3-4 KJV

Jesus, too, felt the sharp sting of betrayal,
rejection, and resistance in His ministry. He
experienced the pain of losing loved ones, like
Lazarus, and even wept (John 11:35 NIV). Despite
the agony, He carried His own cross, bruised and
wounded, a profound demonstration of His love for
us. Have you ever felt the weight of carrying your
own cross, knowing it leads to sacrifice? Have you
been burdened with others' issues, later becoming the
sacrifice for their problems? Have you trusted

someone, believing they were a confidant, only to find yourself the talk of the town when disagreements arise?

Daily, I encounter couples and singles eagerly preparing for marriage, yet many are fractured like I once was. While I haven't been married myself, I've counseled married individuals through ministry. I've also shared dreams of a future with partners, only to see my heart shatter like a wine glass hitting the wall. People carry silent burdens; their appearance betrays the turmoil within.

Opening up about these struggles requires convincing from the Holy Spirit. Whether for personal healing or ministry, the Holy Spirit guides when and how to share heartbreak experiences. I draw courage from the Spirit's conviction and appreciate colleagues who also trust me with their stories.

Broken Paths, Redeeming Grace

In the symphony of life, heartbreak encounters compose the haunting notes that resonate within our souls. These are the poignant melodies played by the pain of betrayal, rejection, and the resistance of destiny.

In this chapter, we delve into the real-life stories of individuals who faced heartbreak and emerged transformed through the redeeming grace of God.

Shylet's Heartbreak Encounter

Psalm 77:3-4 KJV "I remembered God, and was troubled: I complained, and my spirit was overwhelmed.

Selah. Thou holdest mine eyes waking: I am so troubled

that I cannot speak."

Shylet, a dear friend since our primary school days, found herself entangled in a disastrous marriage. A union marked by abuse, deceit, and the haunting shadows of fear.

2

As we explore Shylet's journey, we unravel the layers of her resilience, the courage to break free, and the divine intervention that led to her restoration.

Dixon's Heartbreak Encounter

Hebrews 12:5-11 NLT "And have you forgotten the encouraging words God spoke to you as his children... But afterwards, there will be a peaceful harvest of right living for those who are trained in this way."

Dixon's tale, narrated from the confines of a prison cell, unfolds the consequences of a life gone astray. Through the darkness of his past actions, we witness the transformative power of God's love and the unexpected redemption that emerged within the walls of captivity.

Shylet's Heartbreak Encounter: A Symphony of Redemption

Shylet's journey epitomizes the resilience of the human spirit when faced with adversity. Her marriage, a canvas painted with the darkest hues, became a testimony to the power of discernment and the courage to break free from the chains of abusive relationships. The echoes of her story resound, urging us to listen, learn, and seek the discernment needed to navigate the complexities of relationships.

Dixon's Heartbreak Encounter: From Chains to Redemption

Dixon's narrative unfolds like a gripping novel, recounting a life marred by crime and despair. As he grapples with the consequences of his actions within the prison walls, his story becomes a testament to the boundless mercy of God. Through the pain of discipline, Dixon's life transforms, illustrating the profound truth that God's love can hasten even the darkest hearts toward redemption.

The Symphony Continues

In the symphony of heartbreak encounters, Shylet and Dixon emerge as instrumental notes, contributing to the ongoing composition of God's redeeming grace. As we navigate the complexities of

2

relationships, may their stories serve as guiding melodies, prompting us to seek discernment, resilience, and the transformative power of divine love.

Pastor Sam's Heartbreak Encounter

Scripture: 2 Peter 2:1–22 NLT

In the sacred halls of what claimed to be a church, I discovered a tale of heartbreak that revealed not every sanctuary lives up to its holy façade. The story of Pastor Sam unfolded during one of my services in Cape Town, South Africa, exposing the shadows that lurk within some religious institutions.

Pastor Sam, an assistant pastor in one of the city's largest churches, approached me with a heavy heart. His recent divorce and a crisis of faith had left him bitter and questioning his divine calling. As we delved into his narrative, it became apparent that the church he served for twelve years was not the haven it pretended to be.

Strange occurrences marred Pastor Sam's marriage, but blinded by trust in his spiritual leader, he dismissed the warning signs. The church's leader began having countless private meetings with Pastor Sam's wife, taking her to events outside the city, all under the guise of serving visiting pastors.

Suspicion turned to shock when Pastor Sam, unbeknownst to them, discovered his leader cohabiting with his wife during an unannounced visit.

Fury gripped him, but the leader justified his actions, citing biblical precedents. Pastor Sam, powerless against his leader, chose to leave. Seeking justice, he brought the matter before the church's ministry leaders. However, to his dismay, they sided with the leader, accusing Pastor Sam of false accusations. He was asked to step down, branded a threat to the leader and the ministry.

This heartbreaking revelation prompted questions about the state of today's churches. Where was the transformative power, the healing, and the deliverance witnessed in the times of Jesus and the apostles? What happened to the church as a refuge and fortress?

Weeks later, as Pastor Sam grappled with his shattered faith, some congregants approached him, revealing they too were victims of the same leader. The ministry was not what it seemed; it involved cultic activities and threats of violence against those who dared expose the truth.

After two years, Pastor Sam's wife, broken and remorseful, reached out to him, ready to confess. Meanwhile, the ministry leader met a grim end at the hands of armed robbers, leaving the church in disarray. The congregants, sensing Pastor Sam's genuine
leadership, urged him to take over.

In reflecting on this tale, I realized not every institution claiming to be a church is true to its purpose. Discernment is crucial, and wisdom should guide leaders to avoid building visions on shaky foundations. Relationships, both personal and

2

spiritual, call for discernment to prevent the compromise of faith.

This story serves as a cautionary tale for all servants of God, urging them to serve faithfully and to seek divine guidance in navigating the complexities of religious institutions.

My Heartbreak Encounters

No matter how your heart is grieving, you should keep on believing, the dreams come true." ~Walt Disney

Winter, my favorite season, had just begun. I earnestly believed that I had moved on and healed from heartbreaks, but little did I know that I was a work in progress. Healing is a process, and it's not an easy journey when you are not ready to forgive. Proverbs 18:14 NLT says, "The human spirit can endure a sick body, but who can bear a crushed spirit?"

2

As usual, I woke up to my 4 a.m. prayer alarm and dragged myself out of bed, heading to the bathroom to brush my teeth. The cold winter morning made it even harder to get out of bed, but it was PRAYER TIME! Being a minister of God's Kingdom, there are days when you feel tired to pray due to life circumstances, but because your spirit has been trained, you pray even when you don't feel like it.

"Prayer is not an option but a necessity," as the late Dr. Myles Munroe once said in his book titled, "Understanding the Purpose and Power of Prayer." After a powerful moment of prayer, my spirit was rejuvenated to start the day. I felt the need to visit my friend, Carol, who had been sending lots of messages that I couldn't attend to due to my busy schedule. I knew she understood that I would create time for her once I got the chance. We all have that special somebody with whom we can go on for ages without talking, not because we don't want to, but due to our busy lives, and that person would still understand. This is how my relationship is with people like Carol. As I scrolled through her

2

messages, I remembered that I also had to pass by the bookshop, as she stayed closer to it.

At the bookshop, I came across a book written by the late Choo Naam Thomas titled "Heaven Is So Real." I had read a few pages at my aunt's house and remembered the intense presence of God I felt. This book was a great addition to my library, and I decided to buy it that day.

So, I headed to Carol's place, thinking it was better to start at the bookshop so that I could head straight home after visiting her. As I walked down the pedestrian road with my earphones in, lost in spontaneous worship, my fingers collided with someone else's on the book, and when I looked up, I was struck with memories of a past love, Colleen. Colleen and I had known each other for two years. He started as my stalker on Facebook, but our communication grew from appreciating posts to being close friends and eventually falling in love. We experienced a long-distance relationship with so much connection and care. However, blinded by love, I made life-altering decisions like dropping out of college to be close to him. Little did I know I was setting myself up for a serious setback and heartbreak. When you fall in love, don't shut down your brains and spiritual senses.

After two years of building our empire and preparing for marriage, Colleen texted one night, asking for a break. There was no specific reason, and he couldn't provide clear explanations. I was left paralyzed and heartbroken.

Back at the bookshop, as I looked at a man who resembled Colleen, memories flooded back. I asked about the availability of the book I wanted, and while the operator checked, the man walked over with another book and a great smile.

I hesitated to give my contact details, unsure how I would get the book to him if it became available. As I contemplated, he approached with a smile, asking for my details. Uncertain, I decided against it and walked towards the exit of the bookshop.

As I walked out, a voice shouted, "Don't you want some coffee with me? Maybe I could get some ideas of how to get charming ladies like you." I looked back, and it was him, and I felt nervous.

"No, thank you, hey," I replied, continuing on my way home.

At 8:30 am, my phone rang. "Hello, Patience speaking, how may I help you?" I answered curiously.

"Good morning Patience, how are you? I was serious about the coffee, no strings attached," the familiar voice responded.

"Sorry, who am I talking to?" I asked intentionally, though I knew it was him, recalling the voice from the bookshop.

"You are speaking to Peter, the guy who almost snatched your 'Heaven Is So Real' book yesterday," he explained.

"Oh, okay. How did you get my contact as I don't remember giving you my number?" I asked with concern.

"I have my ways," he replied humorously, and I started to get annoyed.

"Sorry, but no thanks. Besides, I have a busy schedule." I then dropped the call, went back into my blankets, and started reading my new novel.

So, I woke up the next day craving coffee. I went to the kitchen only to find that I had run out of coffee in the house. I decided to go to a coffee shop and later finish my assignments. I took a walk to the coffee shop, and as I sat there, I saw two love birds enjoying their coffee, reminding me of my past with Colleen.

The wounds were taking time to heal, and I struggled to accept that we were not meant to be. Love life can affect our hearts deeply if we are not careful in choosing the right partner. Since the breakup, I pushed away every gentle guy, trying to protect my heart. The two love birds in the coffee shop made me look back, and suddenly, tears started running down my face. I quickly left the coffee shop. My eyes clouded with tears, and I couldn't see clearly. I kept bumping into people. To my surprise, I bumped into

3

the same guy with the naughty voice, Peter. "Patience, why are you crying?

Who has hurt you, my dear?" he asked while picking up my keys and books. I wiped my tears, gave him a cold shoulder, and continued walking home as fast as I could, eager to lock myself in and sob on my pillow.

He spoke louder, but I couldn't hear what he was saying. When you're broken, everything around you sounds irritating. The pain you carry when broken is unbearable, as Proverbs 18:14 says, "The spirit of a man will sustain his infirmity, but a wounded spirit who can bear?" Feeling bad about how I reacted to Peter, who might have been trying to be caring, I felt useless and broken. Maybe he was attempting to reach out to me as a friend. I decided to sleep, but my mind had been affected at the coffee shop. I rolled in bed, tears gushing out. I realized I had not healed from my breakup with Colleen, even though I thought I had moved on. It was still a work in progress.

3

These heartbreaks were not of romantic nature but were equally impactful, cutting deep into the core of my being. It seemed like a season of trials and tribulations, where the pain flowed from different sources.

As I lay in bed, I reflected on the events of the day. My encounter with Peter had stirred up emotions I thought were long buried. The wounds from my past heartbreak with Colleen were still raw. The facade of moving on had crumbled, revealing the unresolved pain beneath. The realization hit me hard – I was not as healed as I believed. The journey of mending a broken heart is a continuous process, and it became evident that I was still on that path.

The tears that stained my pillow were silent witnesses to the emotions I hadn't fully dealt with. The next morning, I woke up with a heavy heart. The memories of love and loss intertwined, making it difficult to navigate through the day. I decided to take a stroll in the park, hoping the fresh air would clear my mind.

As I walked among the trees and listened to the birds' melodies, I pondered the complexities of love. The park, once a place of serenity, became a backdrop for my internal struggle. The echoes of laughter and shared moments with Colleen haunted me, and I questioned whether I would ever find love again.

Amidst the internal turmoil, I received a text message. It was Peter. Despite my initial cold response, he expressed genuine concern about my well-being. His words were comforting, and I felt a twinge of gratitude for his unexpected kindness.

We decided to meet for coffee, not as a romantic gesture, but as two individuals sharing the commonality of heartbreak. As we sat in the corner of the coffee shop, sipping our drinks, Peter shared his own stories of love lost and lessons learned. It was a cathartic experience, realizing that we were both on a journey of healing. The conversation with Peter became a turning point. I understood that healing wasn't a solitary endeavor. Sometimes, unexpected companions appear on the path, offering solace and understanding.

Peter, with his caring demeanor, became a friend – a companion in the process of stitching together the fragments of a shattered heart. Days turned into weeks, and Peter remained a supportive presence. Our encounters shifted from coffee shops to meaningful conversations about life, faith, and the intricate dance of love. The wounds of the past, though still present, began to lose their sting.

In the process, I learned that healing doesn't follow a linear trajectory. It's a mosaic of moments, each contributing to the overall picture of restoration. The journey with Peter taught me the value of vulnerability and the strength found in shared experiences.

As winter faded into spring, so did the lingering pain in my heart. The chapter of heartbreak, once dominant, began to close. I embraced the warmth of newfound friendship and the gradual emergence of hope. My personal heartbreak encounter became a

3

testament to the resilience of the human spirit. While scars remained, they became markers of strength rather than symbols of defeat. Life, with its twists and turns, had a way of surprising us with unexpected allies on the path to healing. And so, with each sunrise, I faced the day with renewed courage, knowing that the journey, though challenging, was forging a stronger, more resilient version of myself. The echoes of past heartbreaks slowly faded, making room for the melody of a hopeful heart, ready to embrace the chapters yet to unfold. One of these heartbreaks came from the ministry I served in. Betrayal and misunderstandings led to a rupture that shattered the unity we once had. As a leader, the burden of guiding others often comes with the weight of their expectations and judgments.

The wounds inflicted in the realm of ministry cut uniquely, leaving scars that needed divine healing. Simultaneously, friendships that I thought were unbreakable started showing cracks. The realization that not all bonds are meant to withstand the test of time hit hard. People changed, priorities shifted, and

3

the pain of losing friends echoed alongside the echoes of past romantic heartbreaks.

In the midst of these challenges, I clung to my faith, seeking solace in the unchanging love of the Holy Spirit. It was during these dark moments that the true essence of resilience and spiritual strength unfolded. The storms may have shaken the foundations of my relationships, but the anchor of my faith held firm.

As I navigated through these heartbreak encounters, I learned profound lessons about forgiveness, resilience, and the transient nature of human connections. The journey of healing extended beyond the romantic realm, touching the very fabric of my social and spiritual life.

Despite the heartaches, I emerged stronger, wiser, and more attuned to the intricacies of the human experience. The chapters of pain were not without purpose; they were chapters of growth, shaping me into a more compassionate and understanding individual.

Life, with its unpredictable twists, continued to unfold. Each heartbreak became a stepping stone, guiding me toward a deeper understanding of myself and others. The scars, both visible and invisible, became badges of honor, testifying to the battles fought and the victories won.

As I stood at the crossroads of past heartbreaks and future possibilities, I realized that the journey of the heart is an ongoing expedition. Love, in its myriad forms, brings both joy and sorrow. Yet, it is through these fluctuations that the tapestry of life is woven, creating a mosaic of experiences that define the very essence of our existence.

"Good morning woman of God. I felt I should tell you that I am pulling out of the ministry. Assign someone else to work on the financial reports," she said in a way that seemed one had already made up her mind.

"Oh, really? It is well. Go in peace and I appreciate all the time I had working with you in ministry."

After this call, I thought to myself, what is really going on with me?

The leader we had just ordained a few days ago had pulled out. The pastor from another branch escaped with some ministry funds. My business partners decided to part ways. Everything was happening so fast, like a movie.

"Good morning, Patience. I am pulling out from the company. I have a lot of commitments to do, so I can't continue doing business with you. Please forward me all the paperwork so I would know the shares remaining for me. Thank you!" It was Mr. Jones, my business partner.

"Okay, Mr. Jones. It was great doing business with you, all of the best," I answered. It reached a point where every day I would just expect sad news, disappointments, and heartbreaks as well. Why were people leaving? God, is there something wrong with me that needs to be fixed immediately so that you can fix me? As I thought to myself deeply, another phone call came through from my restaurant manager.

4

"Good day, Ma'am. The shop is on fire. We lit the gas stove wrongly after it had spent the whole night fuming the shop.

Everything is burnt down now, I don't know if you can come over quickly?" "What???? You mean my shop is on fire?" I couldn't believe my ears.

"Yes, Ma'am. Please come over, we need you." I was numb for a while, then I dropped the call and I just sat on my couch out of words or any action to take. I was just powerless and hopeless. Everything was just happening
so fast.

After a raw breakup, it can feel like nothing will ever be the same again with many sufferers reporting feelings of depression, anxiety, exhaustion and even insomnia. I had to live with this dilemma of heartbreak from the people I had given access to my heart. I had to accept that some people had torn me apart and left me in pieces.

Friends, siblings, ministry congregants, and also ex-boyfriends had crushed me and pushed me away. Were they the only wrong people?

Is there something I might have done that made them get annoyed with me? What really went wrong? These are the thoughts that ran into my mind. I still had no understanding at all.

CHAPTER 3

LIVING WITH A BROKEN HEART.

"I am feeble and sore broken: I have roared by reason of the disquietness of my heart."

Psalm 38:8 KJV

L iving with a broken heart is like breathing through cracks. It's like you are walking around naked with a half-empty soul tied down by a rope that still belongs to another. It is a slow and torturous process that suffocates us and causes us pain. No one has died because of a broken heart, but something inside dies. The trust, the emotions, the attitude, the space for our loved ones again. I was broken, I was crushed, and I felt like I was in my own world. Where is God when it hurts like this? I was bitter, and I had anger problems. When interacting with people, I would react instantly. This was due to a short temper. I thought I was protecting myself from future heartbreaks from various people, yet I was hurting myself more. Trust me, my brother

4

and my sister, no matter how you truly love the person, don't hold on because you think there will be no one else. There will always be someone else.

You've got to believe that you are worth more than being repeatedly hurt by someone who doesn't really care. You need to believe that someone will see what you are really worth and will treat you the way you should be treated. As time went on, God started giving me strength and wisdom. I had to live in an understanding that I am rejected, but God had not rejected me. I had to live in wisdom on how to handle people who had wounded and crushed me. Even if they are to come back today, I can gladly say, I have forgiven them.

I pray for them and I still love them. God started making me see how he overlooked my weaknesses and my trespasses, and He still loved me. I have moved on, and those who left and are not coming back.

I have understood that some people don't have to be kept in our lives, especially if they are just a small chapter in our lives, though they will still exist. Holy Spirit, thank you. So this has taught me that in life, one does not need to be attached too much to people, especially those you minister to. I also learned that not everyone is supposed to understand you, no matter how they wrongly judged you.

Family rejections made me understand that it is only God who proves your innocence; never try to prove your innocence to people. In my life, I encountered many heartbreaks from all types of relationships I had with people. Friends, siblings, business partners, church congregants, and all other different relations. This resulted in me living a life of bitterness. I committed myself to people's success, but the end was not good at all.

I believe in people's gifts and I have a passion to unleash and promote those gifts. It has not been an easy thing to do something for someone out of sacrifice and still, they can't see the effort you are

4

putting. I have stretched myself out for people who were not grateful.

People who never understood that I had to gather all the strength to make everything look blissful. Have you ever reached yourself in debt trying to please someone?

I understood that in life, you don't do things for people expecting them to be grateful or appreciate you. I have seen people who preach what they only heard or something they are not sure of, but I am writing this book out of my experiences.

Heartbreak encounters I had were not only for my love life but for even the people I thought were close friends, close siblings, close relatives, close spiritual relatives.

I encountered heartbreaks from people I never thought, in any single moment, they will be history in my life. I don't only blame them, but I also blame myself at some point.

4

Some might have not liked my reactions towards them. Some might have been wrong connections who were not meant for me, while some were just seasonal people, and their season to go had come. I had so many mistakes I made and it affected me. I had a weakness of trusting people too much.

I would meet a person today and not hesitate to open up my personal and private issues. I would pour myself out, seeking attention to be comforted and pitied. I never imagined people would change to be like strangers. As I navigated through the aftermath of these heartbreaks, I discovered the importance of self-love and setting healthy boundaries. It became clear that healing starts from within, and I needed to embrace my worth without seeking validation from others.

God's love became my anchor, reassuring me that I am fearfully and wonderfully made. Forgiving those who caused the heartbreaks wasn't easy, but it was a crucial step towards my healing journey. Holding onto resentment only weighed me down, and I realized that true freedom comes from letting go. The lessons from these experiences became stepping

4

stones to personal growth, resilience, and a deeper understanding of the complexities of relationships. In the process of rebuilding my life, I learned the value of discernment in relationships. Not everyone who enters your life is meant to stay, and some connections are only transient.

Recognizing toxic patterns and distancing myself from negative influences became a priority. Despite the scars that remained, I embraced the beauty of imperfection. Life unfolded in unexpected ways, and I found strength in vulnerability. The journey of living with a broken heart transformed into a testament of courage, strength, and the capacity to love again. As I reflect on the chapters of pain and heartbreak, I understand that life's tapestry is woven with threads of joy and sorrow. Each experience, no matter how challenging, contributes to the masterpiece of our existence. The broken pieces of my heart were mended not by avoiding love but by learning to love myself and others more authentically.

4

The echoes of past heartbreaks may linger, but they no longer define me. I stand as a resilient soul, shaped by the storms and healed by the grace that surpasses all understanding. The journey continues, and with each step, I embrace the uncertainty, knowing that my heart, once broken, now beats with a rhythm of hope and renewal.

CHAPTER 4

REDEFINING RELATIONSHIPS

Proverbs 18:24, "A man [that hath] friends must shew himself friendly: and there is a friend [that] sticketh

closer than a brother."

To Adam, God was both the spiritual and physical Father, which is the first relationship we see in the Bible. Later on, God had a heart for mankind, and He felt his loneliness. He felt the need for a helper. In other words, we relate to being helped or to help. Every relationship carries benefits and must be of value. Any relationship you have that does not improve, you run away from it. In Genesis 2:20, Adam gave names to all cattle, fowl of the air, and every beast of the field, but for Adam, there was not found any help for him. Every relationship has to meet your standards. It has to bring out the real you. You can't relate with abusive people and shine out there. At times, we put ourselves in trouble just to please people who don't even care for us. Obviously, we are vulnerable to heartbreaks and high blood pressure. When Eve was brought to Adam, Adam was in a position to define Eve, though Eve failed to meet the definition he was given by entertaining the devil instead of helping Adam overcome the devil (Genesis 2:23).

How have you defined people around you? After the storm of splitting has settled, all you need to do is to find a common ground and a new perspective on relationships. I understood that some relationships come to an end for different reasons and some of those reasons can be mightily hurtful. So, I had to be wise in my next perspective.

In mankind-to-mankind relationships, we need to be conscious, as these relations have led to many heartbreaks, suicides, depression, and so on. We need to know how to relate to every person we meet in our daily lives. Not everyone is your friend, and not everyone is your sibling, neither is everyone your father or mother.

In our everyday lives, we are crushed, we are broken, and if we are not careful, it will destroy us. I have had so many relationships in my life, and some I didn't define well and some I did. In life, there are different relationships, and one has to lead his or her life. Heartbreak hurts, and it's something one cannot bear. If you've ever had a broken heart, you will probably understand why that term is used - it feels like your heart is torn into pieces and it's disintegrating. Sometimes you can put on a happy face because the show must go on, but then the night comes.

You find yourself lying in bed, tears streaming down your face and the weight of the hurt heavy on your chest. Wondering if you will ever make it to the other side of the pain whilst you feel completely alone. Days, months, and years passed as I accepted living in the state of brokenness. I had allowed matters of my heart to keep piling every day with no one to pour out to. I had no one to trust again as a confidant, as everyone seemed the same. I lived with bitterness, hatred, anger, stress, and emotions within my heart. Another day, as usual, I woke up for my 4 am prayer then the Holy Spirit whispered in my ear, *Psalms 20:7 - "Some [trust] in chariots, and some in horses: but we will remember the name of the LORD our God." John 14:16, "And I will pray the Father, and he shall give you another Comforter, that he may abide with you forever."* These scriptures were put in my heart.

The Holy Spirit gave me an understanding of how reckless I was with myself. I had put so much trust in my friends, siblings, forgetting that the Bible says, *Psalms 118:8 - "[It is] better to trust in the LORD than to put confidence in man."* I had really gone out of track by not allowing the Bible to continue to be my guide. I went through depression, which reached the extent of attempting to commit suicide. I thought no one cared. No one loved me.

I felt useless and not helpful. Why?

Everything was breaking down. People were just walking in and out of my life as they want. Some would leave me in a state of feeling used.

Proverbs 18:14, "The spirit of a man will sustain his infirmity; but a wounded spirit who can bear?" You should know that when you are living with a broken spirit, no one can bear to stay close to you. No one can be able to keep walking with you. I had to realize that I have to heal. I had to get my heart to mend in order to interact with people and mostly, God. You can never go to people and win their hearts when you are broken but if you go to God.

Psalms 51:16, "For thou desirest not sacrifice; else would I give [it]: thou delightest not in burnt offering. 17 The sacrifices of God [are] a broken spirit: a broken and a contrite heart, O God, thou wilt not despise." After foolishly thinking I could mend my broken heart on my own, I finally came to my senses and turned my pain over to the Lord. As always, time and time again, God proves how great He is.

5

Only God can stand a broken spirit. God alone can mend it, not people. People can just edify the state of your heart, be it a merry heart or a broken heart.

Mankind relationships are just there to edify negative or positive thoughts on your heart. I then decided to proceed with my 4 am prayers to understand the whisper of the Holy Spirit concerning the state of my heart. I still enjoy the 4 am prayer, and each time I do, my day is supernatural. I encourage you to also engage in morning prayers.

Psalms 63:1, "O God, thou [art] my God; early will I seek thee: my soul thirsteth for thee, my flesh longeth for thee in a dry and thirsty land, where no water is;" This has been my favorite scripture in my morning prayers. It really touches my heart. It also contributed to the healing of my heart. When you are living in the world of broken hearts, you attract broken things too. You attract broken issues in people's lives. The heart is the most sensitive part of mankind's life and it needs to be given healthy standards for you to live longer. I have been in the hospital due to heart attacks, heart failure, and low blood pressure. These diseases were being caused by depression.

A broken heart attracts diseases too. You can't live healthily while living with a broken heart. As I embraced the process of healing, I learned that rebuilding oneself after heartbreak is a journey that demands patience, self-reflection, and spiritual guidance. Just as God provided Adam with a helper, I sought assistance from a higher power, realizing that true restoration comes from divine intervention.

The scriptures became my solace, guiding me toward a deeper understanding of the divine love that surpasses human comprehension. I discovered that trusting in God rather than solely relying on human relationships is the key to enduring strength. Psalms 118:8 echoed in my heart, reminding me that placing confidence in the Lord brings a stability that surpasses any human assurance.

Proverbs 18:14 resonated deeply within me – a wounded spirit is a heavy burden. It became clear that attempting to carry the weight of a broken heart alone only leads to further despair. The sacrifices God desires are not burnt offerings but a contrite heart, a heart willing to surrender to His healing touch.

Reflection

After foolishly thinking I could mend my broken heart on my own, I finally came to my senses and turned my pain over to the Lord. As always, time and time again, God proves how great He is. Only God can stand a broken spirit. God alone can mend it, not people. People can just edify the state of your heart, be it a merry heart or a broken heart.

Encouragement

Mankind relationships are just there to edify negative or positive thoughts on your heart. I then decided to proceed with my 4 am prayers to understand the whisper of the Holy Spirit concerning the state of my heart. I still enjoy the 4 am prayer, and each time I

5

do, my day is supernatural. I encourage you to also engage in morning prayers.

Psalms 63:1, "O God, thou [art] my God; early will I seek thee: my soul thirsteth for thee, my flesh longeth for thee in a dry and thirsty land, where no water is;"

This has been my favorite scripture in my morning prayers. It really touches my heart. It also contributed to the healing of my heart. When you are living in the world of broken hearts, you attract broken things too. You attract broken issues in people's lives. The heart is the most sensitive part of mankind's life and it needs to be given healthy standards for you to live longer.

I have been in the hospital due to heart attacks, heart failure, and low blood pressure. These diseases were being caused by depression. A broken heart attracts diseases too. You can't live healthily while living with a broken heart.

5

CHAPTER 5

TIME TO HEAL

Matthew 27:46, "And about the ninth hour Jesus cried with a loud voice, saying, Eli, Eli, lama sabachthani? That is to say, my God, my God, why hast thou forsaken me?"

Jesus knows the feeling. When He hung on the cross, exposed, beaten, and betrayed by those He loved, He felt very alone. As hard as the situations are, we still have comfort in the word of God. We still have a way out.

He never promised a life without heartache, but His word gives us promises to hold on to when such times occur.

Reflection: In the midst of our deepest wounds, we find solace in the understanding that Jesus, too, experienced the agony of betrayal and isolation. As we navigate through our own heartbreaks, we draw strength from the promises embedded in His word.

The Bible becomes a refuge, providing assurance that, despite the pain, there is hope. Jesus, the Ultimate Healer: We also need to consider Jesus as the source of our healing—the doctor of all doctors. There are many types of doctors, and we all relate to them according to the conditions of our health. You can't go to see a dentist if you have an eyesight problem, neither can you go see an optician if you have a broken leg; you will need a physiotherapist for your broken leg. Some people don't see the need to go for medical check-ups until they get worse; it is being reckless with your health.

Personal Revelation: I made the same mistake several times. I had a bad condition with my heart and would only go when I was critical. This also affected my spiritual life. I was no longer in a good state physically and spiritually. I had to see the great need to see a doctor.

I realized I needed serious medical attention but not to mankind doctors. I had to ask God to be my physician.

Spiritual Check-Up: When your inner self is affected, it also affects your physical body, mostly your heart. My heart was broken, and no man seemed to heal this. I had to ask God to be my heart Doctor. I needed Him to fix me. "Fix me, Jesus, fix me, fix me on my humble cry o-o-oh o-o-oh fix me." I could sing this song over and over again. It was a song I needed at that time.

Claiming God's Promises: I began to remind God of His promises. How He promised us a new heart, not a stony heart. I needed a revival with Him. I needed a bond for my relationship with Him. Oftentimes, we only realize the need for Jesus Christ when we are on the verge or the sickbed. We realize how we need Him when we are critical. This is not right at all; I thought to myself.

I thought about how I had been reckless with my health and how I had not seen the importance of living a healthy spiritual life and physical life. Awakening: I have seen the importance, and I want Christ to forgive me for allowing toxic issues to access my heart. For allowing poisonous people to access my heart. I had to take instruction from my heart Doctor. It is what you give access to your body that has the power to access it.

It is the relationships you have that can determine whether you have a healthy soul or a sick one. My heart Doctor was Jesus Christ. He was the only one who could restore me. He is the only one with the capacity to pick up my broken pieces and put them in the right position. I had a need for Him. I didn't want Him, I needed him. I needed Him to start this journey with me. The journey of living a healthy life.

CHAPTER 6

A NEW HEART

Ezekiel 36:26, "A new heart also will I give you,
and a new spirit will I put within you: and I will
take away the
stony heart out of your flesh, and I will give you a
heart

of flesh."

One early morning during my usual 4 AM to 6 AM daily devotional prayer, I found myself sobbing, leaning on my couch. There are times where you would fail to figure out what really went wrong with you. You ponder every idea before God in tears saying, "What did I do Lord to deserve this?" I had to ask God, "Why me?" "Where did I miss the mark?" "What is the root cause of all this pain?" "Was I really called into ministry or I just assumed because of how your gifts were manifesting on me?" I sobbed and sobbed, trying to figure out issues that had no one to answer. I felt like I needed a spiritual surgeon to place me in surgery so I could recover.

Seeking Spiritual Surgery

I started asking God to be my surgeon and had strong thoughts that something must be done. If you have ever been in surgery, you will understand what I mean. My situation was so critical to a point where if I had tolerated it, I would be history by now. I felt the damage inside of me which no physical doctor could attend to and come up with a solution. I remember this prayer being a prayer, full of tears and sobbing. All I was just doing was groaning with no utterance like what the bible says, *"Likewise the Spirit also helpeth our infirmities: for we know not what we should pray for as we ought: but the Spirit itself maketh intercession for us with groanings which cannot be uttered." (Romans 8:26-27 KJV)*

A Prompted Scripture

I had no one to hear this, and I didn't want anyone to hear it. I was also looking at how my disciples would take me, for if they were going to see me in tears like this. At the end of the prayer, a scripture was prompted into my heart.

Psalms 51:10, "Create in me a clean heart, O God; and renew a right spirit within me. 11 Cast me not away from thy presence and take not thy holy spirit from me. 12 Restore unto me the joy of thy salvation, and uphold me
[with thy] free spirit."

Decision for Spiritual Surgery

No doctor has ever demanded you to come to the surgery but you as an individual take that step to get your treatment from the doctor. The woman with the issue of blood understood that Jesus was her surgeon.

6

No matter what people were saying, all she wanted was to get treated. As the scripture was prompted, I had to take that decision that I needed to be in a spiritual surgery.

A Heartfelt Prayer

"And Jesus went with him, and a large crowd followed

Him and pressed in around Him [from all sides]...She thought, 'If I just touch His clothing, I will get well.' Immediately her flow of blood was dried up, and she felt in her body [and knew without any doubt] that she was healed of her suffering..."Daughter, your faith [your personal trust and confidence in Me] has restored you to health; go in peace and be [permanently] healed from your suffering." (Mark 5:24–34 AMP)

Spiritual Warfare and Healing

We are in a spiritual warfare, and every battle that we go through attracts wounds which if no proper attention is given, we are vulnerable. I can say that I had reached a critical stage with my heart and I

6

needed a surgeon to attend to me. I sobbed and spoke louder on that scripture, on how I deeply wanted a new heart. I made a firm decision that no matter the position I was in, I needed a surgeon.

A Decisive Prayer

"Father God, create in me a clean heart. A heart that is not toxic or poisonous. Lord God, grant me a heart that is not broken. I ask for a new heart within me. A heart that is not bitter.

A heart that is not hardened. Lord God Almighty, my heart is heavy. I need a new heart to start afresh with you, Jehovah. I am begging you this early morning, Daddy. My state is critical, it is beyond repair and it will be useless if I go to physical surgeons but I have realized You are the only remaining Surgeon who can resolve this. Lord, I am tired. I am tired of living in grief, pain, heartbreak, and depression. I am tired. I need a restful heart.

I need a peaceful heart. Oh, Lord God Almighty, create a new and clean heart inside of me...."

6

Supernatural Encounter

I went silent for a moment and I felt that peace and that steadfast love of God in me. It was the kind of peace and love I felt the day I received the baptism of the Holy Spirit some 15 years ago. I felt it, and I didn't want to leave that atmosphere, so I just lay there saying God I am in the surgery. I had decreed that I was not going to leave His presence without a clean and new heart. As I lay parallel on my mat, I began to experience some strange but peaceful things. I felt belonging and restful. Thank you, Holy Spirit.

I felt the spiritual machines in the surgery doing some mending. I could feel it, suddenly, I was caught up in a deep sleep.

The Dream of Healing

I dreamt like I was in surgery in a theatre. I could see the doctors surrounding me and I couldn't feel the pain. I was numb. I knew an operation was taking place but I failed to understand how and what had made me get into the theatre.

I could hear their voices and the sound of their scissors and all the metal machines. So, a man who had a white coat stepped in and looked in through where the operation was taking place and just said, "It's done!" Suddenly, I just woke up and saw how time had moved. I had been lying there for about three hours and I started praying, thanking God like someone who had got a bursary.

The Joy of a Renewed Heart

My spirit was dancing. I could tell myself I am indeed free and happy. I could sense something great. I felt all the great things coming. I felt something new. I felt free. I was super excited.

I had received my new heart and I didn't want anything to pollute my God-given new heart. After my encounter with the spiritual surgery with God, I felt a new heart stored in me. I could feel it, and I was so certain that something supernatural had happened to me. I had no time to entertain evil thoughts inside me. The time to entertain heartbreak, oppression, and rejections was gone. I started focusing on my vision. I started paying attention to the will of God, not of people. Everybody has the right to live a healthy life. Everybody deserves a healthy heart. Praise God, Hallelujah! Christ loved me and gave me a healthy heart.

I was given a new heart.

Living with a New Heart

When you have a new heart, it's easy for you to forgive. It is so easy for you to move with God alone, even if people walk away. The things and people you give access to your body and soul can improve or affect your health. The people you trust with the issues of your heart can also improve or affect you. So, it is vital for one not to keep piling issues.

I have learned to pour out my issues before God. I have learned to go before God first and confide in Him before going to friends and relatives. My encouragement to you is that a new heart exists and only God is the best surgeon. No matter the worst you have gone through, there is a God in heaven who grants new hearts. A new heart carries new things which are not toxic.

You need to see to it that you maintain your new heart. See to it that people don't pollute it. Avoid the wrong company.

CONCLUSION

*Let us hear the conclusion of the whole matter:
Fear God, and keep his commandments: for this is
the whole duty of man*

Ecclesiastes 12:13 KJV

In the tapestry of life, as you navigate the chapters of heartbreak, let Christ be your Heart Doctor, your divine Cardiologist. If you find yourself broken, rejected, and feeling like an outcast, know that Christ is the only Doctor capable of restoring your heart. As you read these words, invite Him into the recesses of your soul, for He longs to encounter you and bring healing to your wounded heart.

You may have traversed many relationships with fellow humans, yet the most important relationship—your connection with Christ—might be missing. Jesus, the Son of God, walked the earth

2000 years ago, offering Himself as the ultimate sacrifice for your sins.

His death was a profound act of love, designed to bear the burdens of your pain, shame, rejection, and oppression. The name "Jesus" means Saviour, signifying His mission to save us from the intricacies of our hearts.

If the testimonies shared here have breathed hope and strength into your weary heart, consider choosing Jesus as your confidant. He is faithful, non-judgmental, and committed to redeeming, sanctifying, and setting you free. Your heart's desire to align with Him is a powerful step toward transformation and the restoration of broken relationships. Embrace the prayer below with a sincere heart, ready for a profound transformation and restoration:

"Lord Jesus, come into my heart. Cleanse me, mould me, and restore me. Create in me a clean heart and renew a right spirit within me. Erase my name from the book of death and inscribe it in the book of life.

Forgive me for my sins, be my personal Lord and Saviour. Be my surgeon, be my everything. Thank you, Jesus, for your love. Amen."

If you've sincerely prayed this prayer, congratulations!

You are now a born-again Christian. Seek out the nearest Christian church led by the Holy Spirit and centered on Jesus Christ as the chief cornerstone. As you embark on this spiritual journey, remember that Jesus is your Heart Doctor. Regardless of what you've been through, He can mend you until you emerge as the best version of yourself.

For feedback, testimonies, or event bookings, feel free to reach out on Amazon Kindle. Whether its conferences, seminars, summits, youth camps, motivational speaking, business seminars, worship concerts, or counseling for marriage and love life relationships, I am here to support and guide you on your journey.

May the grace of our Lord Jesus Christ, the love of God, and the sweet fellowship of the Holy Spirit be with you now and forever. Amen.

www.ingramcontent.com/pod-product-compliance
Lightning Source LLC
Chambersburg PA
CBHW071837020426
42331CB00007B/1763